INTRODUCTION

WHAT IS A POISON FROG?

Poison frogs, poison-arrow frogs, dart-poison frogs...This is a book about a group of tiny to small frogs from the Central and South American rainforests. Their often brilliant colors and attractive patterns long have made them desirable to advanced terrarium hobbyists, but until recently they were just dream frogs

(genus *C*... species) and the strange stinking Skunk Frog (*Aromobates nocturnus*). Dendrobatids are closely related to the rainfrogs, family Leptodactylidae, one of the most confusing and large families of American frogs. Usually a dendrobatid can be told from a rainfrog or a treefrog (family Hylidae) by looking at the tips of the fingers.

D. GREEN

A fairly typical poison frog, the Three-striped Poison Frog, *Epipedobates trivittatus*. Most poison frogs are attractively colored but not gaudy.

for the average hobbyist with a limited pocketbook and just one or two terraria. But just what are poison frogs and why, for that matter, am I not calling them "poison-arrow" frogs like almost everyone else?

To put them into perspective, our frogs represent some 65 species in the family Dendrobatidae, which contains about 175 described species. The dendrobatids include not only the true poison frogs, which produce distinctive toxins or poisons in their skin, but the rocket frogs

Though all these frogs tend to have discs at the end of the fingers and toes, in the dendrobatids the tops of the fingertips have two small raised humps, the scutes, that are just about the only visible character to let the average hobbyist distinguish a dendrobatid.

Not all dendrobatids, nor all poison frogs for that matter, are colorful, but some are among the most beautiful of all frogs, with gaudy patterns of red, yellow, and even green and blue. Dendrobatids are active during the day, and the most colorful species often are not at all shy, venturing about in the open and in plain sight of predatory snakes, birds, and small mammals. The rocket frogs are the least colorful dendrobatids and lack distinctive skin toxins. The true poison frogs with the most potent toxins tend to have the brightest colors and most "out-going" personalities.

It seems likely that true poison frogs have developed brilliant colors to warn predators that they are distasteful. Such warning colors are termed aposematic by scientists and occur in many different types of animals, especially in the tropics. Poison frogs have few predators, and for good reason. Instances are known where a snake has been seen to bite into a poison frog, only to immediately release it (spit it out, actually) and begin to rub the lip scales on the ground while writhing about in obvious pain. Occasionally the snake predator became comatose for several minutes or even hours if it bit into a particularly toxic species of poison frog, while the frog itself just hopped or walked away virtually unharmed except for a few shallow bite marks.

The presence of skin toxins has directed the lives of poison frogs. Because they lack predators they can be active during the daytime, allowing males to establish long-term territories from which they call to attract females. They lead long lives once they mature (the Harlequin Poison Frog has lived at least nine years in captivity), and specialized care of the eggs and often the tadpoles lead to a high percentage of eggs producing adult frogs. Females of most species seem able to lay small batches of eggs every few weeks throughout the wet season or perhaps throughout the year, which

Poison frogs are noted for their tremendous color variations within one species. This Strawberry Poison Frog, *Dendrobates pumilio*, from an island off Panama lacks most of the bright red typical of its species. Many hobbyists like the unusually patterned forms. Photo: R. D. Bartlett.

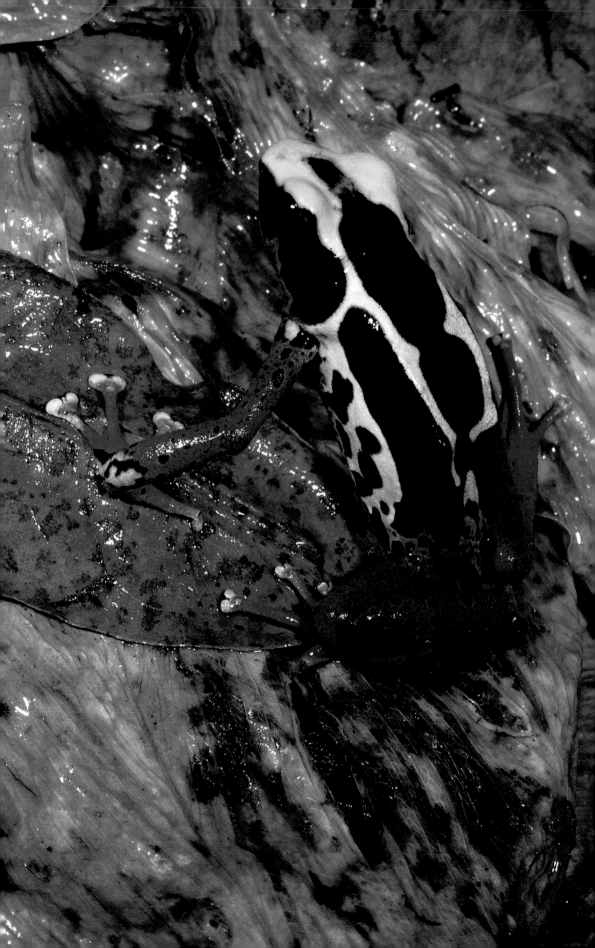

means that poison frogs can occur in tremendous numbers in suitable habitats (though many species seem to be rare for unknown reasons). At least some species can maintain stable populations over several years while being extensively "harvested" for the pet trade. Poison frogs are among the most successful of tropical frogs in many regards, yet most species have very small geographical ranges.

Among the species with small

darts, not bows and arrows. Though some Amerindian tribes from the Amazon basin probably were using bows and arrows before Europeans entered their realm, all available evidence indicates that the various Colombian tribes who use poison frog toxins for hunting and warfare have always used blowguns. The traditional common name for the poison frogs, **poison-arrow** frogs, thus is based on a misconception and was replaced by some writers with

Lithodytes lineatus, a poison frog look-alike of the family Leptodactylidae.

J. P. BOGERT

ranges are three *Phyllobates* restricted to western Colombia. Contrary to legend and repeated statements in both popular and scientific literature, these three species—*P. aurotaenia, bicolor,* and *terribilis*—are the only dendrobatids proven to be used by local Amerindians to tip the darts for their blowguns. Yes, I said blowguns and

Facing Page: A male (notice the very large toe pads) Dyeing Poison Frog, *Dendrobates tinctorius,* one of the best choices for beginners. Photo: M. Panzella.

the more correct name **poison-dart** frogs in the early 1980's. Very quickly, however, several writers began to invert the order of the words in the names to the grammatically more accurate **dart-poison** or **arrow-poison** frogs.

Of course, it could be pointed out (and it has been) that only three of over 60 species of these frogs actually are used to poison darts, which seems to make the entire "poison-arrow" bit a poor choice for a common name. For the past few years Dr. C. W. Myers (the leading American worker on these frogs) and

P. FREED

Rocket frogs like this *Colostethus marchesianus* are non-toxic relatives of the poison frogs.

his colleagues have been using the more biologically correct and simpler term **poison frogs** for the dendrobatids that produce skin toxins. I like this name—it's short, simple, and distinctive—and recommend that it be used consistently to replace older names.

OK, enough. Let's get on to the frogs. This little book is designed to introduce you to the poison frogs both in nature and in the terrarium. If you read through the whole thing, you should be able to keep and breed at least three or four common, captive-bred species. As you look at the pictures you will develop an ability to recognize the common species of poison frogs in some of their many disguises. More importantly, I hope you will remember that these spectacular little frogs are children of the rainforests in which they evolved and live today. When the rainforests disappear, as is likely over great parts of the tropics by the beginning of the next century, the frogs will disappear with them. The frogs you might breed will never be reintroduced to a natural habitat, but they might end up being among the last individuals of their species. Enjoy the poison frogs for the little jewels they are but never forget their bleak futures.

The Phantasmal Poison Frog, *Epipedobates tricolor*, has a truly fantastic blend of colors. Photo: R. D. Bartlett.

Golden Poison Frogs, *Phyllobates terribilis*, may have skin poisons strong enough to kill an adult human on contact. Photo: A. Norman.

The "bulls-eye" pattern of the Harlequin Poison Frog, *Dendrobates histrionicus*. Photo: R. D. Bartlett

A QUICK LOOK AT THE SPECIES

No one really knows how many species or kinds of poison frogs exist, but as I write this there are 65 scientifically described, named, and of poison frogs, but as an interested hobbyist you should known what species are potentially available to you now or perhaps in the future. I've

Some Ruby Poison Frogs, *Epipedobates parvulus*, are beautiful little animals, but many are rather dull like this one.

generally accepted species. A species is very hard to define, but in a general way it is a distinctive group of animals (or plants, for that matter) that look enough alike to be recognized as distinctive and share a common gene pool—i.e., they breed together (exchange genes) to produce offspring like the parents. Although many of the poison frogs display a tremendous amount of variation in colors, patterns, and sizes, no subspecies are recognized by scientists today—a poison frog is a full species or it is not formally recognized.

I'm not going to bore you with detailed information on all 65 species used a simple code to give you an idea of what to expect in the terrarium:

A= availability to average hobbyists: c, commonly seen; s, seldom seen; u, rare or unknown in general commerce.

K= keepability in very broad terms: s, relatively simple, given basic knowledge; i, keepable by moderately advanced hobbyists with some experience; d, difficult even for experienced hobbyists; u, unknown or at least few or no records of terrarium experience.

B= breeding ease given healthy adults in proper terraria: o, often bred, even by beginners; s, seldom bred by average enthusiasts; d, difficult or virtually impossible, even the experts give up; u, breeding seemingly unreported in the terrarium.

An asterisk (*) indicates that captive-bred stock is now or was

THE GENUS *DENDROBATES*

Poison frog genera are hard to tell apart from external characters, but generally *Dendrobates* species are moderate to large in size for the group (20 to 50 mm from tip of snout to vent), have greatly expanded

R. D. BARTLETT

Metallic gold stripes are an attractive feature of the Golfodulcean Poison Frog, *Phyllobates vittatus*, a species found only in a small area of Costa Rica on the Pacific Coast.

recently available, though you might have to search for it. Some of these species may be available only by exchange with specialist breeders. Be sure you receive a guarantee that the stock really is captive-bred and not just said to be captive-bred...it does make a difference.

If you want more details on any species, see my larger book *Rainforest Jewels* for full coverage of just about everything known about poison frogs.

fingertips, and have the first finger shorter than the second finger. Color patterns generally lack a bright stripe from the base of the thigh (the groin) to the armpit. There are 26 species recognized in the genus.

Polka-dot Poison Frog, *D. arboreus.* Au; Ku; Bu.

Green and Black Poison Frog, *D. auratus.* Ac; Ks; Bo.*

Blue Poison Frog, *D. azureus.* As; Ki; Bs.*

Biolat Poison Frog, *D. biolat*. As; Ki; Bs.

Rio Santiago Poison Frog, *D. captivus*. Au; Ku; Bu.

Brazil-nut Poison Frog, *D. castaneoticus*. Au; Ku; Bu.

mysteriosus. Au; Ku; Bu.

La Brea Poison Frog, *D. occultator*. Au; Ku; Bu.

Strawberry Poison Frog, *D. pumilio*. Ac; Ks; Bd.

Rio Madeira Poison Frog, *D.*

The Ecuadorean Poison Frog, *Epipedobates bilinguis*, is a close relative of the Ruby Poison Frog but has bright, clearly marked yellow spots on the thigh and arm.

P. FREED

Red-headed Poison Frog, *D. fantasticus*. As; Ki; Bs.*

Splash-backed Poison Frog, *D. galactonotus*. Au; Ku; Bu.

Granular Poison Frog, *D. granuliferus*. Ac; Ks; Bd.

Harlequin Poison Frog, *D. histrionicus*. Ac; Ks; Bd.

Mimic Poison Frog, *D. imitator*. As; Ki; Bs.*

Pasco Poison Frog, *D. lamasi*. As; Ki; Bs.

Lehmann's Poison Frog, *D. lehmanni*. As; Kd; Bd.

Yellow-banded Poison Frog, *D. leucomelas*. Ac; Ks; Bo.*

Maranon Poison Frog, *D.*

quinquevittatus. As; Ki; Bs.

Red-backed Poison Frog, *D. reticulatus*. As; Ki; Bs.*

Sira Poison Frog, *D. sirensis*. Au; Ku; Bu.

Splendid Poison Frog, *D. speciosus*. As; Ki; Bu.

Dyeing Poison Frog, *D. tinctorius*. Ac; Ks; Bo.*

Yellow-striped Poison Frog, *D. truncatus*. As; Ki; Bs.

Brazilian Poison Frog, *D. vanzolinii*. Au; Ku; Bu.

Zimmermann's Poison Frog, *D. variabilis*. As; Ki; Bs.*

Amazonian Poison Frog, *D. ventrimaculatus*. As; Ki; Bs.*

THE GENUS *EPIPEDOBATES*

Epipedobates is another available genus of poison frog, though its species are seldom seen on the open market. Externally the genus can be distinguished by the combination of a first finger that is as long as or longer than the second, only moderately expanded fingertips, and the absence (with rare exceptions) of dorsolateral stripes that run from the eye to above the base of the thigh, not into the groin at the base of the thigh. Unlike the similar *Phyllobates*, colors are seldom metallic. Most of these

Red-backed Poison Frogs, *Dendrobates reticulatus*, are little gems with bright red backs and even a bright red chin spot.

species have teeth, but that can be hard to determine unless you can hear the pinhead crickets scream.

La Planada Poison Frog, *E. andinus*. Au; Ku; Bu.

Sky-blue Poison Frog, *E. azureiventris*. As; Ki; Bs.*

Pleasing Poison Frog, *E. bassleri.* As; Ki; Bs.*

Ecuadorean Poison Frog, *E. bilinguis*. As; Ki; Bs.*

Bolivian Poison Frog, *E. bolivianus.* Au; Ku; Bu.

Marbled Poison Frog, *E. boulengeri.* As; Ki; Bs.*

Cainarachi Poison Frog, *E. cainarachi.* Au; Ku; Bu.

Palenque Poison Frog, *E. erythromos.* Au; Ku; Bu.

Espinosa Poison Frog, *E. espinosai.* As; Ki; Bs.*

Brilliant-thighed Poison Frog, *E. femoralis.* As; Ks; Bs.*

Lutz's Poison Frog, *E. flavopictus.* Au; Ku; Bu.

Niceforo's Poison Frog, *E. ingeri.* Au; Ku; Bu.

Manu Poison Frog, *E. macero.* Au; Ku; Bu.

Confusing Poison Frog, *E. maculatus.* Au; Ku; Bu.

Myers's Poison Frog, *E. myersi.* Au; Ku; Bu.

Ruby Poison Frog, *E. parvulus.* As; Ki; Bs.*

Peruvian Poison Frog, *E. petersi.* Au; Ku; Bu.

Spot-legged Poison Frog, *E. pictus.* As; Ks; Bs.*

Blue-breasted Poison Frog, *E. pulchripectus.* As; Ki; Bd.

Tepui Poison Frog, *E. rufulus.* Au; Ku; Bu.

Silverstone's Poison Frog, *E. silverstonei.* As; Ki; Bs.*

Emerald Poison Frog, *E. smaragdinus.* Au; Ku; Bu.

shorter than the second and the fingertips greatly expanded. Patterns are varied, ranging from narrow stripes to solid bright red coloration over the entire body, but no species has yellow bands or dots across the

R. S. SIMMONS

Very similar to the Golfodulcean Poison Frog, the Lovely Poison Frog, *Phyllobates lugubris*, comes from the Atlantic Coast of Costa Rica and Panama.

Phantasmal Poison Frog, *E. tricolor.* Ac; Ks; Bo.*

Three-striped Poison Frog, *E. trivittatus.* Ac; Ks; Bo.*

Sanguine Poison Frog, *E. zaparo.* Au; Ku; Bu.

THE GENUS *MINYOBATES*

Only two species of the really tiny frogs in *Minyobates* are occasionally available, and most of the species have never been kept in private terraria. The structure of the hands is like *Dendrobates*, with the first finger

back. Adults range from about 15 mm to 21mm or so, truly miniature frogs.

Collins's Poison Frog, *M. abditus.* Au; Ku; Bu.

Alto del Buey Poison Frog, *M. altobueyensis.* Au; Ku; Bu.

Cauca Poison Frog, *M. bombetes.* Au; Ku; Bu.

Yellow-bellied Poison Frog, *M. fulguritus.* As; Kd; Bd.

Blue-bellied Poison Frog, *M. minutus.* As; Kd; Bd.

Andean Poison Frog, *M.*

P. FREED

Epipedobates femoralis is named the Brilliant-thighed Poison Frog because of the bright red "flash mark" at the base of the thigh that helps startle possible predators.

The Harlequin Poison Frog, *Dendrobates histrionicus*, comes in many different colors and patterns. This marbled pattern certainly is not one of the most attractive.

R. D. BARTLETT

opisthomelas. Au; Ku; Bu.

Demonic Poison Frog, *M. steyermarki.* Au; Ku; Bu.

Green Poison Frog, *M. viridis.* Au; Ku; Bu.

Santander Poison Frog, *M. virolinensis.* Au; Ku; Bu.

groin, at least in juveniles (*P. terribilis* and sometimes *P. bicolor* bury the dorsolateral stripes in bright pigment completely covering the back of adults). The thighs usually are covered with a fine speckling of bright greenish or bluish pinpoints. All the colors appear metallic.

B. KAHL

Rarely seen in the hobby but much in demand at high prices is the Blue Poison Frog, *Dendrobates azureus.* Restricted to southern Surinam, the species is on various endangered species listings and hard to obtain legally.

THE GENUS *PHYLLOBATES*

The few species currently placed in *Phyllobates* have the first finger as long or longer than the second and have the fingertips only moderately expanded (as in *Epipedobates*). All five species have bright yellow or orangish dorsolateral stripes from the eye to the top of the thigh, not the

Kokoe Poison Frog, *P. aurotaenia.* As; Ki; Bs.*

Black-legged Poison Frog, *P. bicolor.* As; Ki; Bs.*

Lovely Poison Frog, *P. lugubris.* As; Ki; Bs.*

Golden Poison Frog, *P. terribilis.* As; Ks; Bs.*

Golfodulcean Poison Frog, *P.*

vittatus. Ac; Ks; Bs.*

Please remember that these codes can apply only in a very general way. Different hobbyists may have different luck with the same species under identical situations. It also is difficult to judge the health of captive

Several of the species listed as unknown all across the board have been kept and bred under laboratory conditions for one or two generations but seem to be unavailable to hobbyists currently. A few species (i.e., *D. lehmanni*) that once were

P. FREED

Though small (only an inch or so), the Ecuadorean Poison Frog, *Epipedobates bilinguis*, is one of the most attractive of the poison frogs. A well-marked specimen like this one not only has bright red tubercles on the back and yellow on the arm and thigh, but a bright blue belly as well. Unfortunately, the small size of many poison frogs makes them difficult to maintain for many generations. Hobbyists always seem to have trouble culturing enough fruitflies to feed their frogs several times a week, week in and week out.

specimens, though generally captive-bred frogs are healthier than wild-caught specimens and will breed easier. Just because a species is commonly available (i.e., *D. pumilio*) does not mean it is easy to breed, as captive-bred specimens of many species are rare or unavailable.

commonly seen are today virtually unavailable because of changes in laws or local exporting procedures, and it must be expected that in the near future many other species that are only available wild-collected will become protected by restrictive legislation.

BASICS OF POISON FROG LIFE

The 65 species of poison frogs, though differing greatly in color patterns, are very closely related. This is shown by their life histories as well as their anatomy. The life histories of about half the poison frogs are fairly well known, and bits and pieces are known about most of the others. From this it is possible to make general statements that will apply to almost any poison frog behavior, always keeping in mind that there are exceptions to everything. Here we go—but remember about the exceptions.

Poison frogs are diurnal (day-active) frogs found on the ground in the leaf litter and debris and on low shrubs and the trunks of trees usually less than 3 or 4 meters from the ground. (Some species, especially those related to *Dendrobates ventrimaculatus*, are found mostly in bromeliads and other plants high in the trees.) They are restricted to warm, humid forests, usually rainforests, especially those where the dry season is short or never occurs. Some species can be found actively searching for their favorite prey, ants, at any hour of the day, while many are most active for an hour or two after sunrise and before sunset or at least before noon. In nature these are ant-eaters (without the snouts, of course) that actively hunt their prey instead of waiting in ambush for it to come to them. In addition to ants, free-living soil mites and springtails are common prey, while many species feed on any tiny beetle and fly larvae they come upon as well. Even adults carrying tadpoles do not hesitate to feed on any ants or mites that they run into.

Males of most poison frogs seem to be territorial. They tend to call from a specific spot on the ground or, more commonly, on a low shrub day after day for several weeks at a time before moving to a new locality. Males of the same species usually space themselves about 3 or 4 meters apart and defend their boundaries from any other males that enter it. These are feisty little frogs, and it is not uncommon for males to wrestle for several hours on the forest floor in territorial disputes. Females possibly have smaller and less defined territories, and they also tend to wrestle with intruders. It is not uncommon for females to fight over males and for males to fight over females. Some species are virtually impossible to maintain in colonies because of fighting among the sexes and between species in confined terraria. Another thing to remember is that females often eat the egg clutches of other females if they run across them, sometimes making it impossible to maintain more than a single pair of frogs in the terrarium if the eggs are left to be cared for by the male.

Males, incidentally, often are hard to distinguish from females. In species with pale throats the vocal pouches sometimes are visible externally as a brownish or grayish wrinkled area at the back of the throat in males. Males usually are 2 to 5 mm shorter than females of the same species from the same locality and generally are more slightly built than females, especially females ready to lay eggs. Only the male poison frog really calls, producing anything from low, soft insect-like buzzes to loud, continuous trills depending on the species. Though poison frog males may have a variety of calls, to most human ears the calls of any one species sound pretty much the same whether the males are defending their territory from other males or reacting to the sight of an egg-bearing female. Females of some species occasionally may make low

Breeding behavior of the Amazonian Poison Frog, *Dendrobates ventrimaculatus*, from French Guiana. (This species is not exactly typical of most poison frogs in breeding behavior.)

A female ready to mate and lay her eggs.

The male, with his inflated vocal sac, calls to attract a female.

The female comes to the male's calling site.

R. BECHTER

buzzes and chips, but they lack vocal sacs and are never really vocal. If several poison frogs are put temporarily in a small container and misted, the males often begin to call and can be identified later if you make color or pattern notes.

Mating usually is associated with periods of high humidity, often the rainy season. (Some species breed all year even in nature.) Male calling intensity increases and there are more fights between neighboring males (none ever seems to get hurt). The calls of a male attract a female, whose egg-inflated body often seems to trigger even stronger calling in the male when he sees her. (Her body shape may serve as a "visual releaser" of sexual activity in the male.) Courtship may take two or more hours and consists largely of the female slowly approaching the male until he leads her on an even slower chase to the egg-laying site (bower). Usually the male moves a few centimeters and the female follows at a distance, then both stop, calling starts up again, the male moves off, and the female follows. Bowers usually consist of dead leaves on the ground in a moist spot (not in the water), often near the protection of a downed tree trunk or heavy moss cover. The bower usually is very dark and not easily seen from above by an observer. The "chase" commonly takes over an hour.

Once at the bower (and sometimes at stops along the way) the frogs may engage in various types of stroking and dancing. Usually the female strokes the male's snout and back, and both sexes may dance around each other in tiny circles while stamping the feet in place. There is a great deal of variation in courtship behavior of the species that have been studied so far, and often there are significant differences among individuals of the same species. Behaviorists have categorized the major types of courtship activities, and some of these are mentioned in *Rainforest Jewels*. Courtship may occupy another hour or even more before the eggs are laid.

Typical frog clasping behavior (amplexus) is absent in most poison frogs, though males of some species of *Epipedobates* and perhaps *Minyobates* may clasp the female about the head (cephalic amplexus). Often the female lays her eggs while the male leaves the bower, fertilization occurring only when the male returns minutes later (sometimes after the female has already left). In some species the frogs assume a position vent to vent during egg laying, the male immediately fertilizing the eggs. In at least a few species the male deposits semen on the floor of the bower, leaves, and the female lays her egg in the semen-wet area. The male may then return to move the eggs around in the area to make sure all are exposed to the sperm.

Generally, males guard or at least tend the clutch of eggs. Most poison frogs of the genera *Dendrobates* and *Minyobates* lay very small clutches of only two to six eggs, though *Epipedobates* and *Phyllobates*

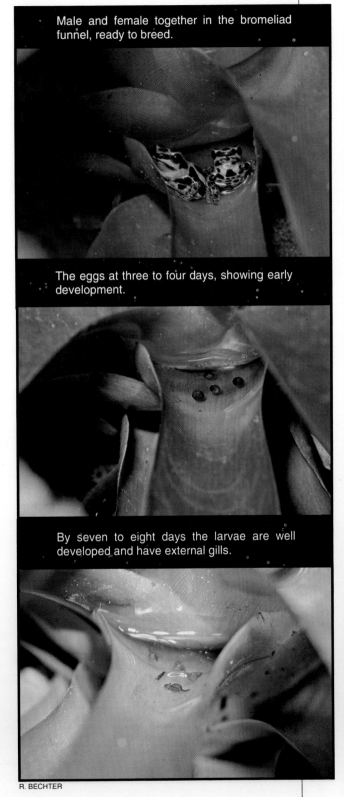

Male and female together in the bromeliad funnel, ready to breed.

The eggs at three to four days, showing early development.

By seven to eight days the larvae are well developed and have external gills.

R. BECHTER

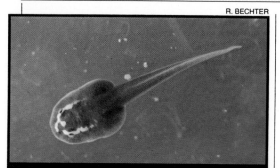

The tadpole of this variety of *Dendrobates ventrimaculatus* has distinct yellow stripes through the eyes.

species may have much larger clutches of one to three dozen eggs. At least in captivity, females may lay every ten days to two weeks month

By the time metamorphosis is almost completed, the Amazonian Poison Frog froglet has the full adult pattern and coloration. In some poison frogs, however, it may take weeks for the pattern and color to develop.

after month, often for more than a year at a time before "burning out," and it seems likely that a similar rhythm exists in nature. The male not only protects the eggs from small predators and other frogs, he keeps the thick jelly around the eggs moist and occasionally moves the eggs around, helping assure that all the eggs get sufficient oxygen. The water he brings to the eggs may either come from his bladder or be trapped on his belly skin while soaking in shallow pools of water.

In reality, this textbook behavior appears to be far from the usual behavior. Often the female tends the bower or both parents check the bower on a regular basis. Another common variant is for the male to tend the clutch for one or two days until the eggs obviously have begun to develop, then disappear for the next ten days, returning a day or two before the eggs hatch. It seems that the male (or female, as the case may be) can identify an individual clutch of eggs, perhaps by smell.

Another variation should be mentioned, this one in egg placement. In the arboreal (tree-dwelling) species related to *D. ventrimaculatus* all the breeding cycle centers about a bromeliad funnel or similar spot that is filled with water. The adhesive eggs sometimes are deposited on a vertical surface, often at the base of a leaf near the water-filled funnel, and there even is a report of eggs and sperm being deposited directly into the water. In some *Epipedobates* it appears that the eggs may be laid on the edges of a naturally occurring puddle or spot of water in a tree trunk instead of a leaf in a relatively dry spot. In the terrarium most frogs adapt to the available bower sites and may not look for natural sites. There are many indications that behavior in the terrarium (including calls and fertilization styles) may not truly duplicate natural behavior patterns.

The eggs hatch in about two weeks (10 to 18 days, the longer period in *Phyllobates* with their large broods), assuming they are fertile and are not eaten by another frog. A day or two before hatching the male (or other tending parent) apparently detects the event to be (by smell?)

and begins to hover near the eggs. As the eggs hatch, the male stretches his hind legs over the clutch and bows his back, forming a trough that the tadpoles can "crawl" up. In species with small clutches the male usually takes only one tadpole at a time, rarely two. The tadpoles have large yolk sacs that sustain them in the heavy moisture-holding jelly remaining from the clutch, so it is not urgent that the parent immediately transfer each tadpole to a water body. In fact, it is not uncommon for a tadpole to be carried about on a parent's back for two to five days, and obviously the tads left at home must be able to survive without attention for longer periods. In at least some species the mouthparts of the tadpole do not develop to a feeding stage until eight days after hatching. In *Epipedobates* and *Phyllobates* species the parent may take a dozen or more tadpoles at a time onto his back, requiring only two trips to transport an entire clutch.

Like most poison frogs, the male transports the tadpoles from the bower to an individual water hole where they mature.

R. BECHTER

The male or other parent gradually transfers all the tadpoles to one or more small bodies of water, where they stay until mature. In most poison frogs the tadpoles are put into either individual water bodies (usually the funnels of bromeliads, water-holding areas at the bases of the branches and stems of various other plants, and holes in standing trees or rotten logs) or just two or three tads share a bit of water. The large *Dendrobates* (*auratus, tinctorius, azureus*) may occur by the dozens in large bodies of water as much as 10 or 15 meters above the ground, it appearing that males have traditional communal spots for depositing larvae. Such large groups of larvae usually exhibit cannibalism, larger tads feeding on smaller tads. Generally tadpoles feed on detritus and algae (thus the use of flake fish food in terrarium rearing) as well as any small insect larvae found with them (especially mosquito larvae, thus the use of bloodworms as a substitute in the terrarium).

Exceptionally, some *Epipedobates* deposit their tadpoles in shallow streams and puddles in ditches. This behavior probably is related to the typically large clutch size of these frogs. Relatively few *Epipedobates* have been well-studied in nature, however, or even raised in the terrarium.

One of the most bizarre exceptions to typical poison frog behavior is that of using food eggs to feed the tadpoles. This behavior seems to be restricted to the species related to *Dendrobates histrionicus* (*pumilio, granuliferus, speciosus, lehmanni,* perhaps *arboreus, occultator*) and is

one of the reasons these species are not suitable for terrarium breeding. The female tends the egg clutch and transports the tadpoles to (usually) individual small water bodies in bromeliads and other plants often several meters above the ground. She then returns at fairly regular intervals (about every two to three days), lowers her rear end into the funnel, and lays an egg that is eaten by the tadpole as the only food. The mother may feed each of her young from 20 to 30 eggs before they mature in about seven or eight weeks. Attempts to duplicate food eggs using chicken egg yolk, cottage cheese, yeast, and various mixtures have been at best marginally

Though poison frogs are small, they are not short-lived. Most are not sexually mature until almost a year old, and they may live for at least five or six years, with ten and more years not unheard of. This young Strawberry Poison Frog, *Dendrobates pumilio*, with good care could easily live for six or more years.

R. S. SIMMONS

P. FREED

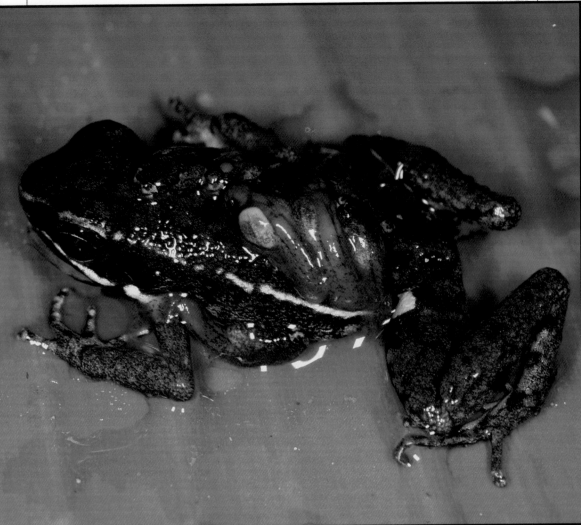

Although most *Dendrobates* species carry only one or two tadpoles at a time, many *Epipedobates* and *Phyllobates* species (such as this *E. pictus*, the Spot-legged Poison Frog) carry six or more tadpoles in one trip.

successful even in the hands of experts. The species related to *Dendrobates ventrimaculatus* may feed their tadpoles on food eggs under certain circumstances, but apparently the tadpoles do not require a constant diet of eggs to mature.

The typical poison frog tadpoles are ready for metamorphosis after two to three months (over 100 days in a few species, and as much as 150 days for some species on obviously improper terrarium diets). Froglets usually are 10 to 15 mm long and take tiny insects such as springtails, mites, and even hatchling spiders as food for the first few weeks. In the terrarium they are peaceful and several can be put in a small moist terrarium and literally surrounded with food. They drown

Poison frogs are difficult to feed when they are young because they require large amounts of very small insect foods. For the first week or two after they leave the water they must have springtails or similar almost microscopic foods, then they become large enough to eat the usual fruitflies. If it survives the first three weeks or so, this Strawberry Poison Frog, *Dendrobates pumilio*, should make a long-lived captive.

easily if not allowed voluntary access to land. Sexual maturity is reached in from eight months to a year (18 months in *Phyllobates terribilis*), and with luck a poison frog should live at least five years and probably ten. In this case small size does not equal a short lifetime...something to remember when you buy your pets.

BASIC TERRARIUM DESIGN

There are as many successful terrarium designs for poison frogs as there are poison frog keepers. As long as the terrarium is large enough to satisfy the territorial demands of males, has heavy cover, remains humid, is warm, and has places to lay eggs, you have a good chance of success, at least with captive-bred large species. Beyond this the terrarium can be as simple or complicated as you wish.

The most simple design incorporates an 80-liter all-glass aquarium (there's nothing wrong with a larger terrarium, but any smaller may not work well). The bottom can be covered with perforated plastic such as "egg crate" (sold in hardware stores as covers for fluorescent light fixtures) that then is covered with fine fiberglass screen. This raises the true substrate above the bottom of the tank and keeps old water out of reach of the animals. (The egg crate material is optional, and the gravel could be put directly on the bottom of the tank, but it does make keeping the tank clean easier.) If you can incorporate a small drain in one front corner of the terrarium it becomes easier to clean out wastewater on a regular schedule, but this really isn't necessary for a basic setup. Cover the screen with small pea gravel and then cover this with sphagnum moss or sheets of living moss to provide a nice backdrop that also will help maintain

PHOTO COURTESY OF ENERGY SAVERS

If you keep plants in the terrarium, you will need the appropriate fluorescent lights.

the humidity in the terrarium. Other substrate materials such as orchid root mix and clean bark mulches work well. A few pieces of cork bark or some branches and broken pieces of flowerpot provide sufficient cover for most ground-dwelling species, but the consensus is that living plants also should be provided.

Putting living plants into a terrarium creates a problem, because plants need light and poison frogs, though active during the day, do not like bright light (being creatures of the dense undergrowth). If you keep living plants, expect to see your frogs less often, perhaps only when food is put into the terrarium. A 4-foot double fluorescent fixture containing at least one light with the spectrum balanced for reptiles and amphibians (see your pet dealer) will provide enough light for most plants that can survive in the moist terrarium. Actually, two daylight white bulbs or one daylight white and one reptile light work just as well—the plants need the light, not the frogs. The lights can be 1 to 2 meters above the terrarium and left on at least 12 hours a day to be sure the plants will thrive.

The plants can be the old standbys, pothos and philodendron, both of which do well in the humid surroundings and are liked as cover by most poison frogs. Prayer plants (*Marantha*) also work well, and a variety of other cheap, attractive plants from the local nursery can be tried. As usual, it might be best to put only potted plants in the terrarium so they are easier to replace if problems develop, but philodendron likes wet roots and will help remove nitrates from the wastewater in the bottom of the terrarium if planted directly into the substrate. Many hobbyists enjoy seeing their frogs use bromeliads (and days, but this is hard to do in the poison frog terrarium. Turn the plant over every week or two to get rid of stale funnel water and refill with fresh water. Always use unchlorinated, soft, nearly mineral-free water to mist the terrarium and the frogs. Spiny plants should be avoided as there are reported incidents of poison frogs ripping themselves open on the spines.

PHOTO COURTESY OF HAGEN

Small plastic aquaria make excellent terraria for froglets as they are always close to their food.

some species, especially *Dendrobates ventrimaculatus* relatives, never really adapt to a terrarium lacking them), which give the terrarium a more tropical appearance. The very common and cheap horticultural varieties of *Vriesea* and *Guzmania* work well, as do smooth-leaved species of *Aechmea*. These bromeliads sometimes produce tight heads of red or yellow flowers, but don't expect this to happen often in the humid terrarium. These bromeliads all have a central funnel that must be kept filled with water if the plant is to survive. They actually should be allowed to dry out a bit every few

The top of the terrarium should be screened for security and about half the top can be covered with a sheet of plastic or plexiglas to help increase humidity while still allowing ventilation. Mist the terrarium thoroughly with tepid water at least every two or three days, and don't ignore your schedule. The humidity should stay above 70%, so adequate ventilation is necessary to prevent bacterial and fungal growth. An undertank heater can be used to keep the temperature at about 24 to 26°C, dropping only two or three degrees at night. Species from high elevations (none of the commonly bred species are high-elevation forms) should have temperatures two to four degrees lower, but actually most poison frogs are quite temperature-tolerant. Increased humidity (daily misting) and a slight drop in temperature may increase male calling and thus successful mating. However, try to avoid water condensation on the walls.

Artificial breeding sites, often called "honeymoon huts," are used for most species and often provide the center of a male's territory. They usually consist of just an inverted flowerpot with a couple of small holes knocked in one or two sides, but many hobbyists prefer to use halved coconut shells for a more natural appearance. As long as the cave is roomy and dark there should be no problem. The hut should be large enough to enclose a petri dish or other very shallow dish that will serve to hold the leaf (usually artificial) on which the eggs are laid. Put just enough clean water in the dish to cover the edges of the leaf, and

PHOTO COURTESY OF TETRA/SECOND NATURE

Living plants need lots of maintenance but plastic plants will do in many situations. Honestly, the frogs cannot tell live plants from good plastic imitations.

PHOTO COURTESY OF RIVER TANK

Though they are not truly aquatic, an arboreal poison frog might do well in a well-designed paludarium setup along with some fish or a newt or two.

change the water at least every two days. The male will soak in the water and thus contaminate it. A shallow bowl of water for soaking can be put in a corner; some pebbles on the bottom help assure the frogs cannot be trapped and drown by accident.

Let's see...have I covered everything? Good substrate, high humidity, drainage (if possible), partially covered tank top, undertank heater or equivalent, plants and lights for them, hiding places, honeymoon huts. Yeap, sounds like just about everything. Let me reemphasize that just because most poison frogs are under 50 mm does not mean that they can be housed in a tiny terrarium. They are territorial and often aggressive, with males in nature spaced at least 3 meters apart, so the

Poison frogs don't need to bask and hate strong lights, so the new dark light heat emitters (which produce no visible light) work best for temporarily raising the temperature in a portion of the terrarium.

more room the better except for the tiniest species that might just disappear in a large terrarium.

TADPOLE FACILITIES

In nature poison frogs take care of their eggs and then put the tadpoles where they will be safe and well fed. In the terrarium, however, eggs left to the care of the parents seldom are tended and often fungus or are eaten. For that reason hobbyists usually remove the eggs to raise them under close scrutiny and then raise the tadpoles. The petri dish is removed from the terrarium an hour or two after laying (remember that fertilization in some species may take place several minutes after laying) and the water is replaced with fresh, clean water that just covers the edges of the clutch. The dish is then covered, kept in a dark place, and checked daily, replacing the water every couple or three days. Some hobbyists put a few drops of methylene blue in the water to help prevent fungus. When the eggs hatch in about 14 days, the tadpoles are transferred to individual aquaria, often by using a plastic spoon.

Each tadpole is given its own aquarium because there is no guarantee that any poison frog tadpole will not become cannibalistic and feed on smaller siblings under aquarium conditions. It may not happen, especially in species of *Phyllobates* and *Epipedobates* that

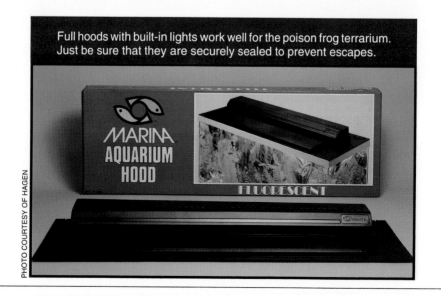

Full hoods with built-in lights work well for the poison frog terrarium. Just be sure that they are securely sealed to prevent escapes.

have large broods raised communally in nature, but why take chances? If you are just raising a single clutch of *Dendrobates*, you should have few problems because each tadpole can be kept in a small bowl of water (a liter or two) and transferred to a new bowl every day or two—cleanliness is essential and must be maintained. Be sure to use unchlorinated water, preferably a bit soft and neutral or nearly so. Most tadpoles take at least 60 days to transform, so you are facing at least 30 water changes per tadpole; don't plan any long vacations!

Many advanced hobbyists and zoo or laboratory breeding programs have mechanized tadpole rearing to cut down on the tedious water changes. There are many different setups used, but the object of all is to put the tadpole aquaria in flowing water to wash away the wastes. A simple method is to use plastic cups (half a liter or less is fine) with two holes cut in the lower base and covered securely with fine mesh. The cups (sufficient for the number of tads being raised) are attached to a floating frame (expanded polystyrene, cork, or some similar substance) so they will remain stable in an aquarium that fits the group of cups. The bottoms of the cups should float about a centimeter from the bottom of the aquarium. In this way the water in the aquarium can be economically maintained at a constant temperature with one heater (25°C or so), yet only one water change is required to clean all the tadpoles. An automatic water changer can be used to efficiently change everything every two days or even more often with even less work, and if you can hook the whole thing together with a small pump to provide a constant flow of clean water through the aquarium, so much the better. Remember...no chlorinated or

otherwise treated water.

FROGLET HOUSING

Because froglets are tiny (usually 10 to 15 mm long) and relatively weak movers, they cannot be expected to find food on their own in a large terrarium. They do not fight, so several (perhaps an entire clutch) can

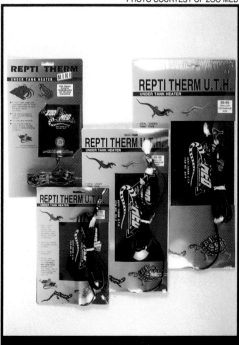

Undertank heating pads are essential for the comfort of your frogs and the plants in their terrarium. Many sizes and wattages are available to suit any setup.

be housed together in a small (10 to 20 liters) terrarium with damp moss on the bottom and plastic over the top to assure high humidity. Froglets will desiccate within hours if the humidity drops. They should literally be surrounded with food of the right size that is easy to both find and catch. After two or three weeks most species will be ready to transfer to a larger terrarium with a good chance of surviving.

PHOTO COURTESY OF FOUR PAWS

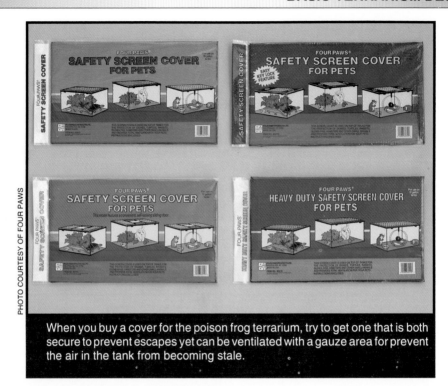

When you buy a cover for the poison frog terrarium, try to get one that is both secure to prevent escapes yet can be ventilated with a gauze area for prevent the air in the tank from becoming stale.

Poison frogs like this *Dendrobates histrionicus* feed on many of the insects and mites that are common in the leaf litter and on low trees. Though they eat mostly ants in nature, terrarium inmates seldom give ants a second look.

R. D. BARTLETT

THE FOODS

Poison frogs need a lots of food. Remember that they are relatively active hunters from a constantly warm climate and you can understand why they have a high metabolism (for a frog, that is). Most keepers feed their frogs every two or three days and let them eat as much obtained by sweeping vegetation with an insect sweeping net (available through many biological supply companies or perhaps can be borrowed from your local college or high school). In the Northern Hemisphere sweeping shrubs and grasses—well away from roads and

Tropical rainforests are teeming with insect-life, especially near watercourses. Poison frogs have evolved to utilize the many different types of ants and mites found in such areas, but they readily adapt to other foods.

as they wish. I've seen reports of obese poison frogs, so obviously it is possible to overfeed, which means you must pay attention to your frogs and cut back a bit if they seem to "inflate" too much after a meal. (Beware you do not confuse overfeeding with egg-carrying; females with eggs must never be underfed. Learn to observe the behavior of your frogs and keep records so you will notice when a female starts to carry.)

The food with the most to recommend it is unfortunately the least used. This is the small insects of all types (flies, beetles, aphids, leafhoppers, true bugs, etc.) that are gardens that might have been sprayed with insecticides or automobile exhausts—from April to October will produce hundreds of tiny insects as well as larger and more aggressive forms that can be removed. Avoid ants and other very hard-bodied insects; though in nature ants are the prime poison frog food, they seldom are taken in the terrarium. Any small spiders and daddy-longlegs in the net also can be fed. Don't put too many insects in the terrarium at once as they could become a nuisance. Small flies and aphids are especially appreciated.

Most hobbyists don't think they

have the time to collect insects, so they instead spend hours inside raising insect cultures. Raising fruitflies (the old standby) and micro or pinhead crickets, sorting them out, and starting new cultures on a regular basis perhaps are the main reasons more hobbyists do not keep poison frogs for long periods of time. You can rapidly find yourself

produces large amounts of yeast. The old culture method was to mash up rotting bananas, mix them with oatmeal or something similar for texture, put the mix in a small bottle that can be stoppered with cotton or a nylon mesh plug, and then pressure cook the whole mix to kill any bacteria and fungi that are present. After the mix cools, live

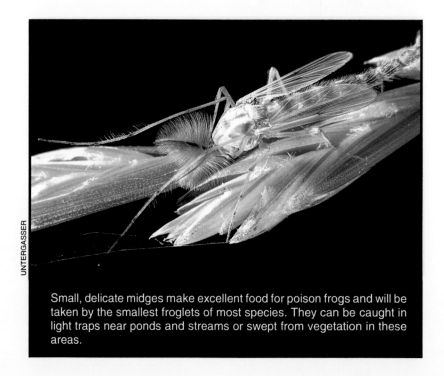

UNTERGASSER

Small, delicate midges make excellent food for poison frogs and will be taken by the smallest froglets of most species. They can be caught in light traps near ponds and streams or swept from vegetation in these areas.

spending more time with the flies than with the frogs. Additionally, disasters always strike food cultures no matter how careful you might be, leading to a desperate rush to find fresh cultures at the worst possible times.

FRUITFLIES

If you ever had a genetics course you've had to raise fruitflies. They are small (under 5 mm or so, depending on species), rather smooth and soft flies that grow in any type of culture medium that

yeast is added, and then in a couple of days a few dozen fruitflies are added. They lay eggs that produce tiny whitish worm-like larvae that burrow through the culture mix and then pupate on vertical strips of blotter paper. The new crop of adult flies emerges within two weeks from when the eggs are laid, depending of course on temperature (the higher, within limits, the faster the life cycle). Today premixed culture media are available from biological supply houses as kits to make it even easier to raise fruitflies. Also, flies with very short and non-usable wings (vestigials) are easily available to lead your ground-living frogs on a merry chase.

Wild fruitflies are everywhere, as you can prove by leaving a banana skin or apple core in your garbage can for a few days. The same simple

rapid fungal growth using this system in the humid confines of a poison frog terrarium, definitely a no-no.

Fruitfly cultures should be started every week or so as any one culture goes bad or runs out of energy within a month, and you will

G. DINGERKUS

Sweeping vegetation with a special insect net will produce a variety of interesting and edible goodies such as small moths for your frogs. Be sure you do not sweep near roadsides or fields where there might be chemical contamination.

technique can be used in a pinch or as a back-up if your cultures start to go bad (they tend to become fungused and also are attacked by mites) and you have to wait a few weeks for the arrival of new stock. Some terrarium keepers have had luck with an even more simple method that shows great promise under some circumstances: Fruit is simply placed in the terrarium, a few adult fruitflies are added, and they breed in the fruit. I've no idea, however, how you would prevent

need plenty of fruitflies. The flies are available at some pet shops, but usually you'll have to buy them from a mailorder live food dealer or through a biological supply house that supplies colleges. They are cheap but take a lot of work.

CRICKETS

The commercial cricket is *Acheta domesticus*, a European species that has been bred for fish bait for years. Almost any pet shop sells adult crickets, and they are available more cheaply in large quantities through mailorder suppliers. However, an adult cricket is almost as large as many poison frogs and more than a match in a fight, so you only want to feed the smallest crickets, so-called micros or pinheads. Though pet shops sometimes sell pinheads, they are

put in each terrarium. A few pieces of lettuce won't hurt. Fiber egg cartons and rolled pieces of corrugated cardboard will provide cover and reduce mortalities. Put about 100 adult (fully winged) crickets in each tank and close the lid. Keep the tanks at a warm room temperature (not below 25°C).

Pinhead or micro crickets are the staple diet of most adult poison frogs. They can be purchased at many pet shops or cultured at home if you have the time and room.

expensive and delicate, and you'll need large numbers. Raising crickets is not exactly a pleasant occupation, but many hobbyists do it from necessity.

First set up at least two 40-liter tanks with about 50 mm of damp sand in the bottom of each and a piece of glass or plastic of the correct size to cover the tank. A shallow saucer of ground-up high-protein dry dog or cat food or a commercial cricket food containing calcium and vitamins (preferred) is

The females (recognized by the long, slender ovipositor projecting from their rear end) start laying eggs in the damp sand within two or three days, 50 or 75 females producing literally thousands of eggs. Most of the adult crickets will die after two weeks (because of old age), so after five or six days in the breeding tank they could be removed to use as food for other reptiles and amphibians you might have—seems like a shame to waste the adults by just letting them die after laying.

The eggs take about 25 to 35 days to hatch at normal room temperatures, at which time each tank will be swarming with minute pale brown crickets, your pinheads or micros. Before hatching starts, you should replace any old food and egg cartons still in the tank with new egg cartons torn into

By the time the crickets are 15 days old they probably will be too large for most poison frogs, so they then can be fed to your other herp pets and fresh breeding tank setups started. Be sure each tank is thoroughly cleaned before reuse and all food and cricket residue are removed. The sand should be stirred and preferably exposed to sunlight

J. KADLEC

Bloodworms, the larvae of various chironomid midges, are excellent food for tadpoles of many poison frogs and can be purchased in many different forms at the local pet shop.

convenient sizes and supply a shallow dish (or plastic yogurt cup lid) filled with cricket food (containing extra vitamins and calcium) plus a couple of small pieces of lettuce. The pinheads will shelter under the egg cartons and, if the cartons are carefully lifted, can be removed intact from the breeding tank to a large jar, where a few taps will cause them to drop off. The collected pinheads should be fed as soon as possible while they still contain food.

and fresh air for at least a month before being used again in order to get rid of cricket wastes. This method is very time-consuming and uses lots of space, as well as requiring rather high room temperatures (unless you used an undertank heater), but it does work. By starting new cultures every two or three weeks you should never be without pinheads, but you'll probably still have to purchase fresh adults since your frogs will eat almost everything you produce.

OTHER FOODS

There are many other things that poison frogs will eat, but none is simple to culture or even purchase and all have really bad problems. Waxmoths are almost impossible to cultivate conveniently, have tough skin, and are very fatty. Mealworms are simply too tough-skinned for poison frogs, even at very small supplemented with "meadow plankton," you should have lots of food of good variety throughout the year.

SUPPLEMENTS

Be sure that all the food you feed is dusted with suitable herp vitamins and calcium powder. Poison frogs are constantly

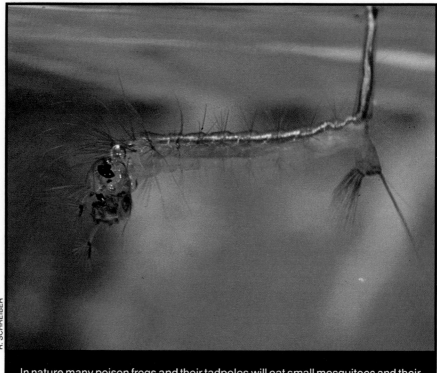

In nature many poison frogs and their tadpoles will eat small mosquitoes and their larvae, a source of food not to be ignored during the summer months.

R. SCHREIBER

sizes. Maggots are disgusting to work with, have virtually unbreakable skin, and have too much fat. As far as I know, no one cultures small spiders for poison frogs, though they should work (but most spiders have relatively slow life cycles). Ants are best avoided, as mentioned earlier. If you stick to fruitflies and micro crickets, producing eggs and sperm in the terrarium, and they need lots of supplements. Poor adult feeding habits may lead to infertile eggs or weak tadpoles even if the adults look good at first glance. The simplest method is to "shake and bake" the flies and crickets by carefully shaking them about in a small plastic bag containing a bit of

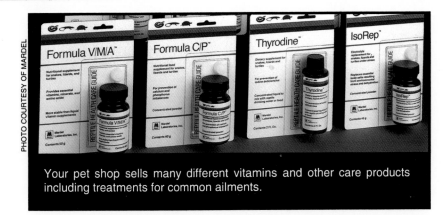

Your pet shop sells many different vitamins and other care products including treatments for common ailments.

finely powdered vitamin-calcium mix. Crickets can be "gut-loaded" by feeding them on heavily vitamin-calcium supplemented food for at least two days before using them as food. Do not overlook these simple steps.

TADPOLE FOOD

The majority of poison frog tadpoles are omnivores; in other words, they eat both plant and animal material, whatever they can get. Most *Epipedobates* and *Phyllobates* tadpoles feed mostly on algae and detritus, so they do well on finely powdered flake fish foods, especially those containing algae. They also eat emulsion foods (vegetable base is best) sold in pet shops for fish fry. Yeast has been used as an emergency food, but it tends to go bad very fast at the water temperatures needed for tadpoles. Some keepers have had good luck with infusoria (green water), but it is hard to maintain green water in sufficient quantities for tadpoles, plus the tads rapidly outgrow the extremely fine foods in infusoria mixes. Boiled chopped spinach is an old standby.

Most tadpoles, especially those of *Dendrobates*, will feed well on worms. They especially like bloodworms (yes, I know these are

the larvae of midges, but to most keepers a worm is a worm), which can be fed fresh, frozen, or freeze-dried as long as they are crushed to release the body fluids and let the tadpoles get through the chitinous skin. Many tadpoles in nature seem to feed freely on young mosquito larvae that share the water bodies with them, an idea for a different food during the warm months. The adults of many poison frogs, by the way, will feed heavily on adult mosquitos, which have soft bodies and are abundant in frog habitats. Male mosquitos don't bite and can be recognized by their bottlebrush antennae if you are worried about escapes into the house.

Tubifex worms may be accepted by some tadpoles, but their high waste contents and questionable origins (most seem to be from the polluted ditches near Mexico City and other high-population tropical cities) make it somewhat dangerous to feed them. Finely chopped earthworms (the smaller the better) sometimes are accepted, but are never used as a staple food.

If you can get a good culture of springtails going (a few handfuls of leaves from the backyard, kept moist and warm, should produce thousands of the almost invisible insects), they can be fed to both

This male Three-striped Poison Frog, *Epipedobates trivittatus*, is carrying a half dozen or so tadpoles to their water hole, where they will mature into tiny froglets in about two or three months. In nature poison frog tadpoles probably get an adequate diet and are produced by parents that have eaten adequate diets, but in the terrarium a frog's diet is always different from that in nature and may be missing essential vitamins or nutrients of which we are unaware. This may be the reason that many terrarium poison frog egg clutches never develop and that so many tadpoles develop slowly, are deformed, or never mature at all. The tiny size of most poison frogs makes them very hard to diagnose and treat when things start going wrong.

tadpoles and froglets. Springtails become trapped at the surface of the water when a handful of leaves containing them is put into a jar of water and then can be skimmed off with a piece of cardboard and transferred to the tadpole aquarium or froglet terrarium (they won't drown). Of course, leaves containing springtails can just be put into a froglet terrarium and left to raise springtails at a natural rate.

Obviously there is no shortage of foods for poison frogs, but all require time to culture or collect.

PROBLEMS

The almost universal problem with poison frogs is their small size. Except for the few large species (*Dendrobates auratus, tinctorius, leucomelas, azureus, Phyllobates bicolor, terribilis,* and a few others), almost all poison frogs are under 25 mm in adult length. Even the largest species will eat only pinhead crickets and tiny waxmoth caterpillars, seldom being able to tackle a full-grown cricket on equal terms, thus the reliance on fruitflies and cricket cultures so essential to maintaining any breeding colony of poison frogs. Additionally, froglets require *really* tiny food, almost microscopic springtails, mites, and the finest of wild-caught insects, food hard to supply during the winter and hard to maintain in numbers over the rest of the year.

A very humid environment is necessary for a successful poison frog terrarium, and that can lead to stagnant air and fungal and bacterial growths. The use of a terrarium with a drain helps prevent the problem, as does the use of sufficient living plants to convert nitrates from wastes and help control the humidity of the air. Plants require sufficient light, usually reptile-balanced fluorescent lights (4-foot units at least a meter above the terrarium and left on for 12 to 16 hours per day). Poison frogs do not like excessive light, so they tend to stay hidden more—in the plants. Compromises may be necessary between healthy frogs and accessibility.

Poison frogs can be kept either as single pairs or small groups, usually of

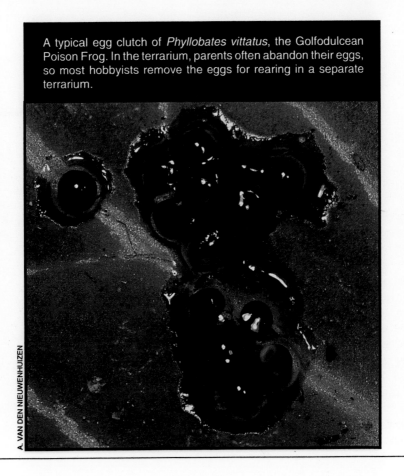

A typical egg clutch of *Phyllobates vittatus*, the Golfodulcean Poison Frog. In the terrarium, parents often abandon their eggs, so most hobbyists remove the eggs for rearing in a separate terrarium.

A. VAN DEN NIEUWENHUIZEN

rates in the terrarium, probably because of insufficient diets. Captive-bred parents tend to have better tadpole survival than do wild-caught parents, perhaps because captive-breeding selects for genes that allow frogs to survive the hardships of captivity. Tadpoles (and adults, for that matter) must be kept spotlessly clean. The water must be changed every day for best results (avoid chlorinated water), which is a lot of work if you are trying to raise a large brood of *Phyllobates* tads. Cannibalism can be a problem if

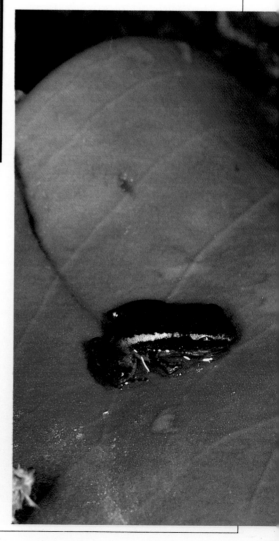

These tadpoles of *Phyllobates vittatus* are showing the usual signs of spindly leg syndrome and will not survive many days after they complete their metamorphosis, if they make it to land at all.

two or three males and up to six females of a species per large terrarium. Though small, these frogs need lots of room—remember that they are territorial and fight. Attempts to let the frogs raise their eggs and tadpoles naturally often result in disaster as the eggs are abandoned by the parent or are eaten by a competitive female.

Fertility rates of egg clutches in the terrarium often are very low, perhaps because the adults are bred at too young an age. Fungus and bacteria quickly attack infertile eggs and may spread to fertile eggs unless removed (probably they are eaten by the parent in nature). Some hobbyists add a few drops of methylene blue or some other fungicide to the egg water and even to the tadpole water.

Tadpoles have very high mortality

the tadpoles are raised in communal aquaria, so usually each tad is raised in its own separate plastic cup covered with plastic wrap and with a few holes punched in the bottom rim to let water flow through to reduce waste levels in the water. A plastic spoon, by the way, is a good method of transferring tads from one container to another during cleaning.

Many tadpoles of *Epipedobates* and *Phyllobates* species mature but something goes wrong with the development of their front legs, which remain small, poorly muscled, and may not even break through the skin.

These pathetic little froglets squirm around on mostly the back legs, cannot catch food (and often seem to have poorly developed mouths anyway), and die naturally in a few days after metamorphosis unless euthanized. This condition, often called "spindly leg syndrome," has no known cause and is not treatable. It does not appear to be genetic or due to tadpole diet, but it has been suggested that it may be the result of an improper diet for one or both the parents (especially the female). The condition also in inconsistent in its occurrence, some pairs producing normal and spindly tads at random in different clutches. Expect the worst and perhaps you will be lucky and get the best. Be sure the female parent, especially, has lots of properly supplemented foods from the moment she becomes a froglet and never let her go without food for more than two or three days.

An adult Phantasmal Poison Frog, *Epipedobates tricolor*, and one of its froglets. In many poison frogs it takes days or weeks for the adult pattern to develop. You can imagine how difficult it is to feed a froglet only half an inch in length. Photo: P. Freed.

R. D. BARTLETT

The Green and Black Poison Frog, *Dendrobates auratus*, has become the beginner's poison frog. Not only is it attractive and inexpensive, but it is captive-bred and readily available at any pet shop that caters to herps. Its larger size makes it relatively easy to feed, and it is fairly adaptable to varying terrarium conditions.

GOOD FOR BEGINNERS

Of the 65 described species of poison frogs, few are actually common in the hobby and available to the average hobbyist. About a dozen species are seen with some regularity in the shops and on dealers's price lists, but of these only five or six are both keepable and perhaps breedable by beginning or moderately advanced hobbyists. Several of these are available as captive-bred stock, which makes them the most suitable for beginners and also for any keeper with an environmental outlook on keeping pets...no animals were removed from the rainforest (at least not in the last four or more generations) to obtain your pets.

GREEN AND BLACK POISON FROGS

I think that beginners should start with one of two species, the Green and Black (*Dendrobates auratus*) or the Dyeing (*D. tinctorius*). Of these, the Green and Black is the most readily available and usually the cheapest, yet it is a pretty and hardy frog of good size that feeds well and usually will breed in the terrarium. So we'll start with it.

Dendrobates auratus comes from southern Central America (Nicaragua to Panama) and northwestern Colombia. A highly variable frog, most specimens in the hobby are about 30 to 32 mm in adult length, but larger and smaller specimens are not uncommon, with very large females commonly exceeding 40 mm and perhaps reaching 60 mm in captivity. Typical specimens are metallic green on a black background, with green bands on the arms and legs and green marbling on the blackish belly. Often the green is replaced by blue, either dull or brilliant metallic, and sometimes it is replaced by tan or dull brown. Hobbyists tend to prefer the blue variants and more advanced hobbyists disparage the green ones,

but I think the common green variety is a truly beautiful animal. Most of the captive-bred specimens in the hobby come from ancestors introduced into Hawaii in 1932 to help control crop insects (unsuccessfully, of course), so your pet probably doesn't even remember the American rainforests.

Over a dozen color and size varieties exist of this species, but few except the green and black and blue and black types are ever available.

An easy frog to keep, provide the Green and Black with a terrarium that is humid, warm, and roomy. Males (which may show a wrinkled trace of the vocal pouch at the back of the throat) are quite territorial and prefer to call from low shrubs, so give them a few branches to make them feel at home. Much wrestling may occur if several males (or females, for that matter) are kept in the same terrarium. Courtship is typical for the group, the female following the male to a bower where she lays usually four to six eggs in a clutch. The male tends the bower carefully for the full 10 to 14 days that the eggs need to develop, and then transfers the tadpoles (usually individually) to a suitable water body. Often dozens of tadpoles representing clutches from several parents are placed in one larger water hole that may be several meters from the ground, but sometimes a single tadpole is placed in a bromeliad funnel or similar plant hole. The tads feed on algae, detritus, insect larvae, and each other (caution: cannibals at work!) for about three months (9 to 15 weeks) before metamorphosing into dull duplicates of the parents. The full color pattern usually develops in two or three weeks. Sexual maturity is reached in about one year, and with luck and good care a typical adult will live for at least four years and perhaps more than ten.

In the terrarium these frogs often

produce infertile clutches for the first few breedings and then settle in to produce a clutch every two or three weeks for several months in a row. A pair will do well, as will a small colony of four to six individuals. The male seldom tends the bower in captivity, so the eggs are removed for incubation in a separate terrarium. Tadpoles should be raised in separate little aquaria because otherwise larger tads will eat smaller tads. They feed readily on both crushed flake fish foods and on crushed bloodworms. Be sure you have plenty of pinhead crickets for the adults and provide vitamin and calcium supplements. Almost all stock of the usual green and black variety is captive-bred, so you really can't

W. P. MARA

Though they are rather large by poison frog standards, Green and Black Poison Frogs still are tiny frogs by most other standards.

R. D. BARTLETT

Dendrobates auratus varies greatly in color and pattern, but most specimens are indeed green and black as in the common name. Hobbyists often prefer odder colors of this species, especially bright blue and black.

go wrong with this species as your first poison frog.

DYEING POISON FROGS

For all practical purposes, this is a larger version of the Green and Black with a different color pattern. *Dendrobates tinctorius* comes from the Guianas of northeastern South America, where every little isolated forest or mountain seems to have its own color variant. At least four common patterns are in the hobby, but typically this is a bright blue (almost blue-black) frog with two broad bright yellow stripes on the back, these connected by crossbands to produce two or three oval blue islands down the middle of the back. The arms and legs are black or deep blue with many bright yellow or black spots. Sometimes the yellow is replaced with white or the two yellow

R. D. BARTLETT

Dyeing Poison Frogs, *Dendrobates tinctorius*, are an excellent choice for the beginning dendrobatid enthusiast with a little more money to spend. These frogs are captive-bred on a commercial scale but still are fairly expensive.

stripes fuse across the back to produce a frog with a solid yellow back on a bright blue-black background—truly striking animals. This is a large poison frog, commonly 40 to 50 mm long, with some females reaching 60 mm. It eats almost anything and can even hold its own against an adult cricket (though this is not suggested). If you look closely, the expanded fingertips of the male can be seen to be even broader than those of the female and more square-cut, but usually it is easier to listen for calling males than guess at such minor details.

B. CHRISTIE

Dyeing Poison Frogs are among the largest species in the group and also among the easiest to take care of in the home. Though they produce only a few tadpoles with each breeding, they breed often if terrarium conditions are good.

Though these are ground-dwelling frogs, they often climb trees and may be found several meters above the ground. As in *D. auratus*, calling territorial males attract females ready to lay. A female follows a male to a bower, lays eight to ten eggs, and has them fertilized by the male a few minutes later. The male tends the bower for at least two weeks and then transfers the omnivorous and sometimes cannibalistic tadpoles to suitable water bodies. Again like the Green and Black, dozens of tadpoles may be placed in one large water hole (often in a hole in a palm tree several meters above the ground) by several males. Tadpoles reach transformation size in about ten weeks and feed on almost anything.

This is an excellent beginner's choice because of its large size, brilliant colors, and common availability. Though not as inexpensive as the Green and Black, it is not expensive by poison frog standards and does well if given plenty of food and the temperature and humidity are maintained at high levels. Wild-caught specimens still turn up in the hobby, but hold out for captive-bred specimens and get a guarantee that your pets are definitely captive-bred. Because of their large size, a pair in one terrarium should be sufficient. This is one of the few poison frogs produced in commercial quantities.

Very closely related to the Dyeing Poison Frog (so-named because of a legend that Amerindians use it to change green parrot feathers to red or yellow ones) is the rare and

R. D. BARTLETT

Dyeing Poison Frogs come in many color varieties, of which those with bright yellow stripes on the back may be the most attractive. The plump appearance of this specimen, along with the relatively small finger discs, indicate it probably is a female.

R. D. BARTLETT

The pale bluish white phase or variety of Dyeing Poison Frog is very common in the hobby. In its rather limited natural range in Surinam and French Guiana, there are many isolated populations of this frog, each differing a bit from its closest neighbors. Additionally, captive-bred specimens may differ significantly in color from their parents.

internationally protected Blue Poison Frog, *D. azureus*, found only in a few localities in southern Surinam. The sides and head of the frog are bright clear blue, while the back is covered with a network of round black spots on blue. This stunning frog often is illustrated but is rarely seen and even more seldom available. Protected under various international endangered species laws, the legal status of all specimens in the hobby has been questioned. A few zoos and laboratories have bred this species in small numbers, and it breeds much like *D. tinctorius*, as might be expected.

Only two to six eggs are laid, and they hatch in 14 to 18 days. The tadpoles, often cannibalistic, transform after two and a half months. Unfortunately the Blue and the Dyeing Poison Frogs have been hybridized in terraria, resulting in the possibility of "impure" gene lines hurting both species in the long run. This is an extremely expensive frog when available and should not be tried by the beginner no matter how tempting.

YELLOW-BANDED POISON FROGS
   One of the more brightly colored large (30 to 40 mm) poison frogs is the

Venezuelan *Dendrobates leucomelas*. The back is black with three broad yellow to yellow-orange bands containing small irregular black spots, the whole frog appearing glossy and even metallic. This frog has been bred in considerable numbers and presently is quite affordable. It is fairly hardy in the terrarium, though not as easy to keep and breed as the Green and Black and Dyeing Poison Frogs. It is almost strictly a ground-dweller, the male calling from the protection of roots and debris. A clutch of about six eggs is laid, and normally the bower is not attended by the male, who leaves after the first day or two and then returns a day or two before the eggs hatch. Often found in cool climates, this frog has a long incubation period of sometimes more than 18 days, but it can tolerate rather low temperatures (24°C). The tadpoles are omnivores like the others we've talked about so far, and they mature in a bit over two months. At first the froglets are dull black and tan, but gradually the bright yellow color of the adult develops.

Shyer than most Green and Black Poison Frogs, the Yellow-banded tends to stay hidden in the average terrarium. Additionally, adults of both sexes fight, making it hard to keep more than one pair in a terrarium. These can be considered minor disadvantages, however, in a relatively easy to obtain species. If you find a few Yellow-banded Poison Frogs at your pet shop and have the money, try a pair (males are smaller and more slender than females, as usual, and call).

AMAZONIAN POISON FROG

Just a brief mention of *Dendrobates ventrimaculatus* is necessary because it and so many of its close relatives have a tendency to appear at random on dealer lists. The several species with finely reticulated arms and legs (small black spots on a bluish white to golden or even greenish background) are arboreal, small (usually 15 to 25 mm long) frogs whose lives center on bromeliads several meters up in the trees of the rainforest. Some have a tendency to lay small clutches of adhesive eggs on vertical surfaces, even the side of the terrarium, as a replacement for the bromeliad leaves they use in nature. The tadpoles are raised in bromeliad funnels. These are not easy frogs to keep or breed, but they can be kept with patience and a bit of experience. Almost all stock is wild-caught, unfortunately. *Dendrobates imitator, fantasticus, variabilis,* and the beautiful red-backed *reticulatus* belong in this group.

R. D. BARTLETT

The hump-backed Blue Poison Frog, *Dendrobates azureus*, is too rare and expensive for most hobbyists. It is considered by many to have the most stunning colors of any poison frog, but personally I think many other species are as or more attractive.

P. FREED

THE PHANTASMAL POISON FROG

Only a single species of the genus *Epipedobates*, *E. tricolor*, is at all common in the hobby, but that species (though small) can be recommended for the beginner with patience. A glossy little (usually 18 to 26 mm long) black to bright red-brown frog, it is marked with a broad yellow to whitish stripe on each side of the body and often a similar stripe down the middle of the back. Captive-bred frogs

R. D. BARTLETT

The tiny Red-backed Poison Frog, *Dendrobates reticulatus*, has a distinctive pattern and is more of a climber than typical poison frogs. Lately it has appeared on the market in numbers, but it is a delicate species not recommended for beginners.

Yellow-banded Poison Frogs, *Dendrobates leucomelas*, are captive-bred in fair numbers and are readily available though moderately expensive. The contrasting colors of the adult are striking.

have tended to change color and pattern from generation to generation, so most frogs seen today are on the reddish side with yellowish white stripes (wild-caught specimens tend to be black with golden yellow stripes), very striking frogs. Unfortunately, the stripes are being lost along with darker coloration. The legs are marked with many yellow spots and stripes.

Usually active only on the ground and on low vegetation, this active frog often wrestles. Males have a loud,

R. D. BARTLETT

Typical adult Yellow-banded Poison Frogs have many small black spots and blotches within the bright yellow bands. In froglets these spots are not developed.

P. FREED

Knowing the proper name to apply to many frogs related to the Amazonian Poison Frog, *Dendrobates ventrimaculatus*, is almost impossible for the average hobbyist. This particular frog, for instance, may actually represent an undescribed species.

In the terrarium, captive-bred generations of Phantasmal Poison Frogs, *Epipedobates tricolor*, tend to modify the colors, becoming more pastel. The remote ancestors of this frog were black with golden yellow stripes.

constant call that can become annoying. The clutches are very large for a small poison frog, often 15 to 25 eggs being laid at a time, with records of up to 40. In captivity a healthy female may lay a clutch every ten days month after month for over a year at a time unless moved to a cooler (22°C) terrarium for a while to break the cycle. The eggs hatch in about 14 days and the tadpoles are all transported by the male in just a couple of trips, clinging to his back and sides. The tadpoles feed on detritus, algae, and other very small prey and supposedly are not cannibalistic; many breeders trust an entire clutch to one

aquarium, which does make rearing easier. Spindly leg syndrome is unfortunately common in this species, leading to high mortalities. Development is rapid, froglets appearing in less than two months. Their small size (10 mm) makes them hard to feed. As I said, this is a colorful frog that has terrarium potential, but it does pose several challenges.

Similar biology is found in the few other species of *Epipedobates* sometimes kept in the terrarium, such as *E. trivittatus*. It also applies in large part to the five species of *Phyllobates*, of which *P. vittatus* and *P. lugubris* sometimes are available and keepable

This "red" variety of the Phantasmal Poison Frog has extremely subdued colors compared to wild-caught specimens. Some captive-bred examples have such watered-down colors that the stripes are not longer distinct.

by relative beginners.

Although it is relatively easy to keep and breed (much like the Phantasmal Poison Frog), the Golden Poison Frog, *Phyllobates terribilis*, is not recommended for the beginner even if gorgeous captive-bred specimens occasionally are available. This is the large (almost 50 mm) and notoriously toxic Colombian species that is quite capable of killing an adult human through casual contact with the skin and certainly could kill any cat or dog that mouthes it. The literature says that these frogs gradually lose their toxicity in captivity and that captive-bred frogs may be relatively non-toxic (by comparison to wild specimens), but the risks are too great. There have been no controlled studies on loss of toxicity in the Golden Poison Frog, and it is best not to trust your life to theories and guesses. Stick to safer species...and remember to always wash your hands after handling *any* poison frog, if you must handle them at all. Never put any poison frog near your face (eyes, mouth, and nostrils absorb toxins very readily) and don't handle frogs at all if you have any cuts on your hands. These little animals are not called poison frogs for naught.

D. GREEN

The true poisonous frogs of the family Dendrobatidae are all members of the genus *Phyllobates*. Three of the five species in the genus look very much alike and are fairly common in the hobby.

A bright-backed variety of *Epipedobates trivittatus*, a variable frog that often is confused with *Phyllobates* species. Photo: M. Panzella.

R. D. BARTLETT

Two of the most common poison frogs in the hobby are wild-collected specimens of the Strawberry Poison Frog (bottom), *Dendrobates pumilio*, in the typical Costa Rican color form, and the Harlequin Poison Frog (above), *Dendrobates histrionicus*, in one of its brighter color patterns.

ALMOST IMPOSSIBLE

I know this will not be a popular chapter with many frog specialists, but I feel that beginners should avoid buying and keeping any specimens of the species related to *Dendrobates histrionicus*. These are the species that feed their tadpoles food eggs, as mentioned in an earlier

P. FREED

Almost as common in the hobby as the Strawberry Poison Frog is the Granular Poison Frog *Dendrobates granuliferus*.

chapter. The female visits her offspring on a regular basis, laying one or two unfertilized eggs in the bromeliad funnel to be eaten by the tadpole. She may feed 20 or 30 (and often probably more) eggs to each tadpole in her clutch during the two or more months needed for development. The tadpoles feed

strictly on these food eggs and do not take any other foods in nature or in captivity. Substitute food mixtures based on chicken egg yolk, cottage cheese, and other guesswork ingredients occasionally allow a tadpole to survive and even transform, but the technique cannot be called a success.

The problem is that three species of this group are very abundant in nature and easily collected. They also are sometimes fantastically colored and are among the most variable of all animals in colors and patterns. The Central American *Dendrobates granuliferus* and *D. pumilio* (the Granular and Strawberry Poison Frogs, respectively) are still collected in large numbers and imported for the pet trade. Though relatively hardy, wild-caught specimens usually are stressed and are almost always damaged or injured to some extent. Most wild-caught specimens fail to adapt to captivity with even the best of care and veterinary assistance and die within a few months rather than living the at least five or six years they would have in nature. Additionally, they are virtually impossible to successfully breed, as explained above. Both species can be seen easily on ecotours of Costa Rica, and it would be better to look at these species in nature rather than behind glass.

The Harlequin Poison Frog is similar to the Strawberry and Granular Poison Frogs, but it comes

R. D. BARTLETT

The beginner must try to overcome the temptation to purchase Strawberry Poison Frogs and their relatives if there is an intention to eventually breed the frogs in captivity. The tadpoles are fed on unfertilized eggs laid by the female directly into the tadpole's water body, a food that has proved almost impossible to duplicate.in the terrarium. If you only want to *keep* a poison frog, these are not bad pets if you get one that is not damaged, ill, or stressed.

from Colombia. Every population differs in color and pattern, but generally they are reddish brown with orange or yellow spots. There may be only one large spot in the middle of the back or dozens of small spots over most of the back and sides. Sometimes the spots join to produce a network or even broken bands. Some specimens are dull brown with darker reticulations, while a few may be touched with green. This species once was imported for the terrarium hobby in large numbers, but most specimens died within weeks or months of stress and injuries. Their tadpoles are almost impossible to raise successfully, as might be expected of a food-egg feeder. In a round-about way, the drug crisis in Colombia may be helping this species, as few are exported any longer. Of course, probably much of its habitat has been converted to coca fields, so I guess all is not bright for the future of this species.

Although slightly off the topic, the tremendous loss of poison frog (and of course other herp) habitat in tropical Colombia, Ecuador, and Peru over the last decade should be mentioned. As more and more farmers have turned to producing coca for the cocaine market, the rainforests have been increasingly burned off for cropland. Additionally, defoliants have been sprayed over wide areas in attempts (probably futile) to destroy coca crops, leading to more destruction of rainforests. Unstable political and economic conditions in large parts of these countries have made access to outsiders very difficult, and collecting and research have been largely confined to the vicinity of parks and reserves. Less and less wild-collected material of all herps becomes available from western South America each year, and there are no indications that things will change in the near future. We can only hope that the rainforests themselves survive, letting our little frogs survive along with them.

R. D. BARTLETT

Harlequin Poison Frogs, *Dendrobates histrionicus*, often are available as wild-caught specimens in the pet shops. As with the Strawberry Poison Frog, do not expect to successfully breed this species in the terrarium. Healthy imported specimens, however, make colorful pets, though they tend to have very high mortality rates.

Mantellas are Madagascan frogs that may bear a strong external resemblance to the poison frogs though they are not closely related. Only a few species of *Mantella*, such as this *M. crocea*, have been described so far, but there are many color patterns going under only a few names, and it is likely that many more species will be described in the near future. They may be kept much like common poison frogs but seldom are bred in the terrarium.

MANTELLAS AND HARLEQUINS

Though they are not poison frogs and are not even closely related to the dendrobatids, hobbyists often confuse mantellas (family Mantellidae, from Madagascar) and harlequin toads (family Bufonidae, from tropical America) with poison frogs. Dealers often contribute to the confusion by selling harlequin toads as poison frogs, a misleading use of names that should stop. Both mantellas and harlequin toads lack scutes on top of the fingertips, and the harlequin toads lack distinct discs on the fingers and toes.

R. D. BARTLETT

Many mantellas have bright "flash marks" on the thighs and at the bases of the arms, much as in some poison frogs. These bright colors serve to distract predators for the few seconds necessary to make a successful escape.

temperature can be a bit lower, 20 to 25°C, cooler at night). They like a planted tank but are shy of light, so the same compromises of lighting versus plant health must be made. Like poison frogs, they eat large numbers of fruitflies and pinhead crickets. Males are territorial, wrestle over females and with other males at territory borders, and are smaller and more slender than females—again like poison frogs.

Almost no captive-bred stock of mantellas is available currently, as these frogs have not proved easy to breed in captivity, or they are too expensive to fill a niche in the pet market when captive-bred. Most stock available is imported directly from Madagascar, where there presently are quotas and seasons on taking these colorful little frogs; they often appear only seasonally on the market, but then may be very cheap to purchase and in almost every shop. Imported specimens often are stressed and may have snout and leg damage as well as intestinal parasites, so check your new purchases carefully. Unfortunately, imported specimens are too inexpensive for most hobbyists to even consider seeing a veterinarian for intestinal worm treatments.

MANTELLAS

These colorful little Madagascan frogs are related to the true frogs (Ranidae) and various Asian allies, though today many herpetologists put them in their own family. Few of the eight to ten recognized species (all very variable) exceed 40 mm in adult length, so they are about in the size range of poison frogs. The colors often are bright as well, orange, yellow, green, blue, and black, another resemblance to the poison frogs. Additionally, they can be kept much like typical poison frogs in a humid terrarium with moss on the bottom and daily mistings (but the

If your purchases stabilize and adjust well to their new terrarium (make it roomy—remember we are dealing with territorial frogs even if they are small), they might breed. A small colony of two males and three or four females seems to work well (actually, everything from one male to one female and four males to one female has been recommended). Males call with a cricket-like chirp and attract females. Every frog in the tank seems to wrestle during mating, but no damage occurs. The female lays a relatively large clutch of two or even three dozen eggs (up to 60 eggs are reported in one clutch) in the dark under leaves and debris at the dry edge of a pond or ditch (in nature) or in a dark flowerpot cave in the terrarium. The eggs develop out of water, and hatching (in ten days or so) usually is timed to occur when rains raise the level of water in the pond or ditch, allowing the tadpoles to escape into the water. The known tadpoles seem to be surface feeders on algae and detritus (powdered flake fish food, for instance), but some may be scavengers. Admittedly, not too much has been published on breeding these frogs in captivity and they are not well known in nature either. The tadpoles can be transferred to shallow cups of water after they hatch. If kept clean, they transform in some six to eight weeks and need tiny foods for the froglets. In captivity mortality rates seem to be excessively high, so probably something is missing from the diet of the adults and/or tadpoles.

HARLEQUIN TOADS

The harlequin toads belong to the family Bufonidae along with the true toads. They also are called stub-toed frogs because of the very short inner finger and toe; there are no broad discs on the fingers and toes. Their classification is in confusion currently, but two genera of harlequin toads are represented in the hobby on occasion,

Above: For many years the only common mantella available was *Mantella aurantiaca*, a brilliant orange to yellowish orange frog. Note the small toe pads indicating that these frogs are typically found on the ground. Photo: P. Freed.

Facing Page: This mantella seems to be related to *M. crocea* (note the black mask, white lip stripe, and unmarked back) but differs in many respects and probably is a different species. Part of the problem with breeding mantellas in captivity may be that sexes are mismatched as to species. Photo: P. Freed.

Melanophyrniscus and *Atelopus.*

Melanophryniscus stelzneri is largely black on the back with bright yellow splotches and a red belly. It lays clumps of eggs in puddles on the forest floor. Termites and other soft foods are preferred. If healthy these toads do fairly well in the terrarium but are hard to breed without using injections of hormones.

The true harlequin frogs generally are flattened, often skeleton-like toads with projecting snouts in many species. They vary from bright golden yellow with or without black spots and chevrons to brilliant red and blue to dull blackish brown. The hind feet are large and have thick webs. These are toads that prefer cool mountain streams with flowing, highly oxygenated water and many rocks and pebbles. When kept in the terrarium they usually are kept too warm and die in a matter of weeks. To be kept successfully, most terrarium specialists prefer a tank setup with flowing water and waterfalls, so a drain and a pump are necessary, putting them out of the reach of average hobbyists.

The large white eggs (about 60 to 100 in number) are laid in strings attached to rocks and branches in the water,

Left: Not all harlequin frogs are brilliantly colored. Some are rather dull, like the yellow and black variant of *Atelopus varius* shown here. Photo: R. D. Bartlett.

Below: When in good condition, adult *Atelopus flavescens* literally glow with a bright pink belly and throat. These can be very expensive frogs to purchase. Photo: P. Freed.

usually on the edges of streams with good flow. The female submerges her head to lay the eggs right at the edge of the water. Harlequin toads have a reputation for staying in amplexus for lets them hang onto the rocks while leaving the mouth free to scrape algae and detritus. The tadpoles are short, broad little fellows with dorsal eyes and short tails. Transformation seems to

P. FREED

This Costa Rican specimen of *Atelopus varius* is more typical of common harlequin frog patterns: brilliant black and yellow above, bright red and black below. It is hard to find any two poison frogs with exactly the same pattern, at least among those commonly available in the hobby. Identifications are a nightmare in this group.

days and even weeks before laying eggs, and newly collected specimens may even stay together in the collecting bag for hours after collecting. The smaller male rides on the back of the larger female. The eggs hatch in about four or five days, the tadpoles escaping into the flowing water, where they attach themselves to rocks and debris on the bottom. Yes, attach—*Atelopus* tadpoles are unique in having a large sucking disc on the belly behind the mouth that take about six to eight weeks but seldom succeeds in the terrarium.

Overall, harlequin toads (except perhaps *Melanophryniscus*) are poor choices for the average hobbyist. They are not hardy, are almost impossible to identify, and do not breed well in captivity. Though they have skin toxins, like any toad, they are not poison frogs, and dealers should stop trying to sell them as dendrobatids for the good of everyone. Colorful, yes; good pets, no.

SUGGESTED READING

H-1102, 830 pages, Over 1800 color photos

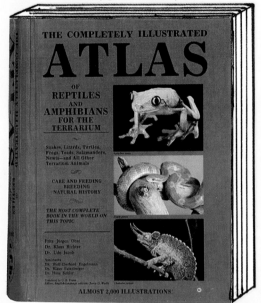

THE COMPLETELY ILLUSTRATED

ATLAS

OF
REPTILES
AND
AMPHIBIANS
FOR THE
TERRARIUM

Snakes, Lizards, Turtles,
Frogs, Toads, Salamanders,
Newts—and All Other
Terrarium Animals

CARE AND FEEDING
BREEDING
NATURAL HISTORY

THE MOST COMPLETE
BOOK IN THE WORLD ON
THIS TOPIC

Fritz Jürgen Obst
Dr. Klaus Richter
Dr. Udo Jacob

ALMOST 2,000 ILLUSTRATIONS!

KD-006 (hard cover), KD-006S (soft cover) 64 pages 230 color photos

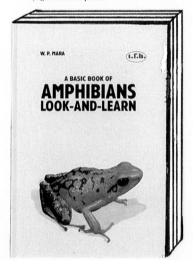

W. P. MARA

t.f.h.

A BASIC BOOK OF
AMPHIBIANS
LOOK-AND-LEARN

TS-182, 192 pgs. 175 color photos

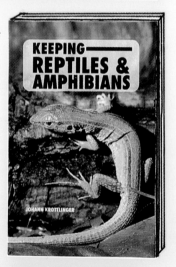

KEEPING
REPTILES &
AMPHIBIANS

JOHANN KROTTLINGER

PS-876, 384 pages, 175 color photos

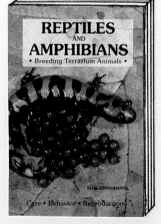

REPTILES
AND
AMPHIBIANS
• Breeding Terrarium Animals •

ELKE ZIMMERMANN

Care • Behavior • Reproduction

H-935, 576 pages, 260 color photos

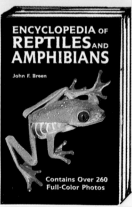

ENCYCLOPEDIA OF
REPTILES AND
AMPHIBIANS

John F. Breen

Contains Over 260
Full-Color Photos

TW-116, 256 pages, 167 color photos

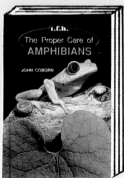

t.f.h.

The Proper Care of
AMPHIBIANS

JOHN COBORN